My Thanksgiving for His Giving

Mother Cantrell
You are a Mother in Zion
You have blessed So Many
Children of GOD.

A FORTY-DAY LENTEN DEVOTIONAL
OF THANKSGIVING

Thank you for Love
and wisdom. God will
continue to bless you.

Dr. Philip Dunston

Pastor Dunston

ISBN 978-1-63575-577-0 (Paperback)
ISBN 978-1-63575-578-7 (Digital)

Christian Faith Publishing, Inc.
296 Chestnut Street
Meadville, PA 16335
www.christianfaithpublishing.com

Printed in the United States of America

Foreword

The late Reverend Dr. Gardener Taylor, quoting one of his contemporaries, once said, "On Sunday mornings the preacher ought to as soon as possible, make his way across the terrain of the biblical text and head to Calvary". With this 40-Day Lenten Journal of Thanksgiving, Reverend Dr. Philip Dunston has done just that. He has, with pragmatism and scholarship, helped us move with dispatch from the season of Advent across the liturgical terrain towards the Lenten Season. Because Calvary is the watershed event of the New Testament, it is timely and additionally refreshing to have this Lenten journal available during this time of indifference and alternative facts that continually polarizes our nation. My friend and colleague of more than twenty-eights years has contributed with this work an absolutely wonderful addition of inspiration and personal testimony woven onto the fabric of the Lord's Truth. It is my extreme privilege to recommend it to every Apostle, Evangelist, Prophet, Pastor and Teacher and Lay Persons in the Kingdom work of our Christ.

Grace and Peace,
Reverend Alfred Walker
Senior Pastor, Bonnie View Christian Church (Disciples of Christ)
Pastor and Chaplain, Baylor Scott & White Health
Dallas, Texas

Acknowledgements

PRAISE GOD FROM WHOM ALL BLESSINGS FLOW

I thank you Lord for the grace to complete this endeavor. Thanks to my beautiful family for their love and support. A special thanks to my parents, my mom Ida for her unconditional love and my dad Philip Sr. for his example of true fatherhood.

Thanks to three of my friends and co-laborers in this spiritual work: Pastor Gregory Taylor, Pastor of the First Baptist Church in Bladenboro, NC, Pastor Alfred Walker, Pastor of the Bonnie View Christian Church in Dallas, Texas and Pastor Wendel Dandridge, Pastor of The Worship Center in Atlanta, Georgia.

Thanks to my spiritual mother Dr. Anne E. Streaty Wimberly for her inspiration and commitment to the body of Christ as Professor Emerita and Director of the Youth Hope Builders Academy at the Interdenominational Theological Center in Atlanta, Georgia.

Thanks to my spirit family, the Friendship Baptist Church in Appling Georgia, where I have been serving as Pastor/Teacher for more than twenty-three years. You all are the greatest inspiration in my life.

Thanks to all my colleagues and professors at Clark Atlanta University, the ITC and North Carolina Central University for the finest education and training in the world.

EVERY GOOD AND PERFECT GIFT COMES FROM GOD

Lent starts on Ash Wednesday, and it ends on Holy Saturday, the day before Easter. Lent is the season of penance and prayer. The forty-day Lenten season is typically a time when we choose to abstain from an indulgence or we practice some measure of sacrificial devotion. Whether you choose to give up something or take something on, what is most important is to ensure that your heart is attentive to the gifts of grace that Jesus has provided by way of his sacrifice on the cross. His act of devotion provided for us forgiveness for sins, the ability to live a full and fruitful life, and a forever home waiting in heaven.

This Lenten devotional will be a unique thanksgiving experience for forty days leading up to the celebration of Easter. At the conclusion of this experience, you will marvel at how often God showed his unconditional love to us, even while he was preparing to go to the cross. Your Lenten experience will become richer and your desire to forget about yourself, and share the love of God with others will increase. As a result of spending this quality time with God in prayer, penance and thanksgiving, your life will grow in joy and gratitude.

A message from President Obama on Ash Wednesday

Today, Michelle and I join our fellow Christians in marking Ash Wednesday. Lent is a season of reflection, repentance, and renewal, a time to rededicate ourselves to God and one another. We remember the sacrifice and suffering of Jesus Christ. We pray for all those who suffer, including those Christians who are subjected to unspeakable violence and persecution for their faith. And we join millions here at home and around the world in giving thanks for this sacred and solemn season that guides us toward the Easter celebration.

A tweet from The Whitehouse: February 10, 2016

Day 1

THE FORESHADOW:
GOD'S CONCERN FOR OUR
HUMAN CONDITION

John 11: 38 - 44

If we were given only one reason to thank God, it could be because of his concern for our everyday human condition. God is concerned about those things that we are concerned about. As I prepared myself for the most traumatic experience of my life, bi-lateral hip surgery, I was blown away at the way in which God was using this experience to show me his divine love and care. Every experience leading up to that faithful day of surgery, God's hand and his peace was present in every preparation. My immediate concern was how to make this transition that was going to require weeks of inactivity as easy as possible for my family, my church, my co-workers, and my community. It was the love of God that sustained me during this difficult time. This is a testimony to the love that God has for each of us.

The death of Jesus' close friend Lazarus was a very traumatic time for him. Although he continued to do ministry, because of his love and concern for Mary, Martha, Lazarus and the family; Jesus was deeply agitated in his spirit. As he journeyed to the family's house and later to the grave site, Jesus gave thanks to his father for what the people were about to receive. His raising of Lazarus from the dead was a foreshadowing of the resurrection experience to come.

Three powerful insights emerge from this death to life miracle: always be mindful of the fact that God is concerned about our human experience. Secondly, God is moved by our faith. And finally, God will raise us up in that great resurrection morning.

Prayer

Father, we are forever grateful for your acts of love and care for us in every situation in our lives. Thank you for being there for us. You promised to never leave us or forsake us. We are thankful because you will be there until the end.

What am I thankful for today?

_____

_____

_____

_____

_____

_____

_____

_____

_____

Day 2

THERE IS POWER IN THE BLOOD

Exodus 12: 1-14

On January 18, 2016, I was scheduled to have hip replacement surgery. For someone who had never been hospitalized, this was a real test of my faith. God made provisions that allowed me to cover all my responsibilities from administrative duties at work, pastoral duties at church, and family responsibilities at home. I was blown away at how God provided for every need.

One of the most intensified moments throughout the entire ordeal was the pre-op experience. The first time you are separated from your family, taken to the pre-surgery room, asked to remove all clothing and disinfect the affected parts of the body, robe yourself in an open-faced surgical robe, and climb into a hospital bed that would be your transportation into the surgical room.

For me, the most powerful instruction was given by the anesthesiologist. He entered my room and told my family how the procedure would commence. He said he would insert a small needle in the base of my spine and once the medicine enters the blood stream, it will travel all over the body. In a few minutes, you will not feel a thing. When we enter the surgical room, it will be pretty busy. You will see men in different areas preparing the room for surgery.

As I entered the surgical room, I was already drowsy from the anesthesia. Five minutes into the room, I vaguely could see men feverishly moving throughout the space. This was about twelve forty-five, Monday afternoon, January 18, 2016. It was about five thirty that evening when I re-opened my eyes. For nearly five hours, I had no conscious awareness that I was in the world.

After coming to myself, I thought about the anointed power in the blood. When God was about to wreak havoc in the lives of the Egyptians, his instructions to the children Israel was to kill a Passover lamb or goat, go throughout their homes and place the blood on their doorposts. And when I see the blood, I will pass over your house and protect you from the plague, so it will not destroy you. The children of God were protected by the blood. The power in the blood is like an anesthesia, no matter how traumatic the experience, it covers you and gives you peace in the midst of it all. There is power in the blood.

Prayer

Father in heaven, today we pause to thank you for allowing the peace of your anointing to shield us when we experience traumatic situations in our lives. No matter what we face, your anointing power can give us rest and peace. Thank you lord for all that you have done.

What am I thankful for today?

_____

_____

_____

_____

_____

_____

_____

_____

_____

_____

Day 3

HE WHO LOVES HIS
LIFE WILL LOSE IT

John 12: 23-26

Just recently, I watched the TV mini-series, "The Fall of Bernie Madoff." Bernie Madoff was the Wall Street mogul who stole billions of dollars from innocent people who trusted him to invest their life earnings. Bernie did not invest any of their money. He stored it away in personal bank accounts and spent it on lavish livings; purchasing yachts, homes, clothes, jewelry, trips, parties, and mistresses. Bernie truly loved the lavish lifestyle. Once his Ponzi scheme was uncovered, Bernie was arrested, convicted, and sentence to one hundred fifty years in maximum security prison. His family was devastated. His brother was arrested, his son committed suicide, his other son was stricken with cancer, and his wife abandoned him after reading about his extra-marital affairs in a book written by one of his mistresses. Bernie lived a life driven by greed, lust, and lascivious living and it eventually caused his demise.

Jesus made an interesting statement just after his triumphal entry into Jerusalem for the last time: he said, "He who loves his life will lose it, and he who hates his life in this world will keep it for eternal life." When indulging in the pleasures of this life becomes more important than serving God and doing his will, the ultimate end can be a life of destruction and death. The Apostle Paul admonishes us, "Do not be conformed to this world, but be transformed by the renewing of your mind that you may prove what is that good, acceptable and perfect will of God." Rom. 12:2

Prayer

Father, thank you for offering to us the opportunity at life eternal in heaven. Because of the sacrifice of your Son Jesus, we do not have to conform to this world, but we can prepare to live in a much greater world where life will be great forever. What a blessing to know that we will live and reign with you in our new home.

What am I thankful for today?

_____

_____

_____

_____

_____

_____

_____

_____

_____

Day 4

The Greatest Enemy, Death, Has Been Conquered

I Corinthians 15:20-28

On Saturday, February 6, 2016, my church family celebrated the home going of a beautiful sister, wife, mother, grandmother, teacher, friend, and family member. She had suffered through so many things in her life, and yet she always remained faithful and strong to the call of God on her life. During the final days of her life, I visited her in the hospital, and heard her praying for her family and our church. She was praying for her pastor and her spiritual family. I thought to myself, this is truly the Christ example that we are called to be. While Jesus was preparing to die on the cross, he was praying for others.

Because of the strength and power of Jesus' prayers, we have been given an opportunity to live with God forever. So when this corruptible has put on incorruption, and this mortal has put on immortality, then shall be brought to pass the saying that is written: "Death is swallowed up in victory." It was on the cross where Jesus uttered, "It is finished," and the final enemy was conquered. "O Death, where is your sting? O Hades, where is your victory? The greatest enemy was conquered. We now have eternal life through Jesus Christ our Lord. That is truly something to be thankful for.

Dedicated to the life of Mrs. Sharon Morrow: Rest in Peace.

Prayer

Father, how can we say thanks for the things that you have done for us? Things so undeserved, but you did them to prove your love for us. The voices of a million angels cannot express our gratitude. All that we are or ever hope to be, we owe it all to Thee. To God be the Glory for the things he has done. (Public Domain)

What am I thankful for today?

_____

_____

_____

_____

_____

_____

_____

_____

_____

Day 5

GUESS WHO'S COMING TO DINNER?

John 13: 18-30

In 1967, a famous actor by the name of Sydney Poitier starred in the classic movie *Guess who's coming to dinner?* The movie was about an interracial couple who were in relationship during a time when inter-racial marriage was illegal in most southern states. The film starring a white woman, Katharine Hepburn, who invited her black husband, Sydney Poitier, to dinner was an instant classic. The audacity of this appearing on the big screen created quite a stir within the motion picture industry.

During a particular season in Jesus life, two pre-crucifixion meals were quite fascinating. The first was at the home of Mary and Martha, the sisters of Lazarus, whom Jesus had raised from the dead. Martha was serving while Lazarus sat at the table with Jesus, and Mary anointed his body with some very expensive anointing oil. Religious leaders quibbled because of the cost of the oil. However, Jesus responded "Let her alone; she has kept this oil for the day of my burial. For the poor you have with you always, but me you do not have always."

The second dinner experience commenced with Jesus washing the feet of the disciples. As they all sat at the table, Jesus lifted some bread and said, "Most assuredly, I say to you, one of you will betray me. It is he to whom I shall give a piece of bread when I have dipped it." And having dipped the bread, He gave it to Judas Iscariot, the son of Simon.

It is profitable for one to be aware of the people that are in your inner circle. It is especially a good thing to know who is sitting at the dinner table with you. The word of God admonishes us to always think on things that are good, true, noble, just, pure, lovely, and praiseworthy. I think these characteristics should also apply to those to whom we invite to dinner.

Prayer

Father, we thank you that you have set the example and given us some guidelines regarding our relationships. All creation is yours and you love us all, but everybody does not need to be invited to dine with us. Thank you for preparing a table for us in the presence of our enemies and our friends. Thank you for being our guest at the table.

What am I thankful for today?

_____

_____

_____

_____

_____

_____

_____

_____

_____

Day 6

LOVE: A NEW COMMANDMENT THAT'S NOT SO NEW

John 13: 31-35

In the early seventies there was a famous husband-and-wife, R&B singing group by the name of Ike & Tina Turner. Although this dynamic duo had a difficult time throughout their marital relationship, they produced some of the greatest rock and roll hits in the history of the music industry. A 1993 documentary film about their lives produced a film entitled *What's Love got to do with it?*

When we think about the ultimate sacrifice that Jesus Christ endured for us, we as Christians believe that he did it because of love. The first and the last message that Jesus delivered to his disciples was, "A new commandment I give to you, that you love one another; as I have loved you, that you also love one another. By this all will know that you are my disciples, if you have love for one another." The only characteristic that really defines a disciple of Christ is the love that he or she has for their fellow human beings. "No greater love has a man than this, that he would lay down his life for his friends."

Prayer

Father, thank you for loving us so much that you were willing to die for us. Please help us to always exhibit divine love to all our brothers and sisters. No matter the ethnicity, social status, religious affiliation, sexual orientation or gender, we are called to love all of your creation. Thank you for loving us.

What am I thankful for today?

_____

_____

_____

_____

_____

_____

_____

_____

_____

_____

Day 7

ETERNAL LIFE?

John 17: 1-5

Do you have eternal life? If you asked one hundred people that question, you would likely receive one hundred different responses. Most Christians are unclear about their eternal resting place. Many of them do not have a clue about the afterlife.

Jesus responded to the question regarding eternal life by saying: "And this is eternal life that they may know you, the only true God, and Jesus Christ whom you have sent." In order to know Christ, you must follow Him. In order to f-o-l-l-o-w him, you must Find him, Own him, Learn of him, Love him, Obey him, and Worship him. Then and only then can you be assured of your eternal salvation. The question is asked, do you have eternal life?

Prayer

Father, we are grateful to have been granted eternal life. You provided that for us through the death of your son, Jesus, on the cross at Calvary. I am glad that I have decided to follow Jesus. As for me and my house, we will serve the Lord and we will never turn back.

What am I thankful for today?

_____

_____

_____

_____

_____

_____

_____

_____

_____

Day 8

DENIAL OF CHRIST DOES
NOT MEAN DEATH

John 18: 15-26

One of the most grievous acts that a Christian can perform is to deny someone who is in need. God has called us to give; to serve and to provide for those who are less fortunate than we are. In fact, God's word admonishes us, "be quick to give and do it with a grateful heart."

Peter was a great example of how God does not destroy us for denying him. Jesus told Peter before his crucifixion that he would deny three times ever knowing him. It happened just as Jesus said. However, immediately after Jesus had finished his mission in the earth, ascended to the father and then returned back to the earth, he had a poignant conversation with Peter. During a sea-side break-fast encounter, Jesus asked Peter, "Do you love me?" Peter answered, "Yes, Lord." Jesus asked him again and even a third time, "Do you love me?" Peter responded, "Lord you know all things; you know that I love you." Jesus knew the heart of Peter, yet it was important for Peter to proclaim that love for Christ "three times." Peter was used by God to preach the inaugural church message that ushered three thousand souls into the kingdom of God. It is a wonderful thing to know that although fear causes us to lose faith, it does not cause God to lose faith in us.

Prayer

Father, thank you for never giving up on us. Even though doubts and fears cause us to deny your power, you always draw nigh to us with your love. You always remind us that we are still loved and counted as usable for your service. Thank you for never giving up on us.

What am I thankful for today?

Day 9

FAITH IN THE RESURRECTION MEANS LIFE ETERNAL

2 Corinthians 5:1-8

This year, I have a greater appreciation for the death, burial, and resurrection of Jesus. I am now convinced that until we are dead to our mortal bodies and raised up into our immortality, we cannot be fully present with the Lord. Paul's statement, "to be absent from the body is to be present with the Lord" has taken on greater significance. Although shaken at first by this revelation, God confirmed this revelation to me in this manner.

God said, "My son you have an earthly father who lives in North Carolina. He is not present with you because you reside in Georgia and he lives in North Carolina. You carry his name, you have his nature, yet he is not present with you." This is how it is with God our heavenly father. We carry his name; we have his spirit, his love, grace and mercy; yet until we are resurrected into our spiritual bodies, we are not present with him. Can you imagine how glorious it will be to actually live in the presence of God, in our permanent house not made by the hands of man?

Prayer

Father, thank you for the faith to experience you without seeing you. Thank you for the faith to believe that you are with us via your spirit, love, mercy, and grace. Thank you for the faith to believe that when this earthly house, this tent is destroyed, we got a building, made by you, that will live eternal in the heavens. What a tremendous blessing to know that one day we will see you face to face, just as you are.

What am I thankful for today?

_____

_____

_____

_____

_____

_____

_____

_____

_____

Day 10

HE IS THE LIGHT OF THE WORLD

John 12: 42-50

How cruel it must seem to live in a world where there is so much darkness. The social ills continue to mount: crime, lawlessness, homelessness, greed, poverty, selfishness, loneliness, racism, sexism, oppression, segregation, terrorism, disease, pestilence, and the list goes on and on. But how refreshing is it to know, as believers that we live in a world and we have the light of the world. Jesus is the light of the world.

Jesus always deflected his light to honor the Father. Jesus said, "He who believes in me, believes not in me but in him who sent me. And he, who sees me, sees him who sent me." "I have come as a light into the world, that whoever believes in me should not abide in darkness." What a blessed assurance and a peace of mind for believers to know that in the midst of the devastating and debilitating darkness in our world, not only do we walk in the light of Jesus, but through him we have been given the ability to let our lights shine. Each day let us walk in the light of Jesus.

Prayer

Father, thank you for sending the light to a dark and dismal world. Thank you for equipping us with the electricity to power up our solar lights and bring focus to a dark world. Jesus, you are truly the light of the world. Help us as your children to let our light shine each day on someone that may be in darkness. Thank you for giving us the light.

What am I thankful for today?

_____

_____

_____

_____

_____

_____

_____

_____

_____

_____

Day 11

JEHOVAH-RAPHA: "THE LORD WHO HEALS"

Exodus 15:22-27

For the next several days, I would like to thank God for the exceptional ways in which he exemplifies his character in our lives. The names of God describe different aspects of his character. Right now, I am particularly in awe of his healing ability. Having lived more than fifty years on this earth, I had never been confined to a hospital room or ever experienced a sickness in my life. Recently, I had to undergo bi-lateral hip replacement surgery. As one might imagine, my faith in God's ability to sustain and heal me through this process was severely tested. The surgical procedure was such a success I was asked by my physician if I wanted to go home the following day. Two days later, I was discharged. Four weeks later, I was nearly completing rehabilitation and ready to return to normal duties in less than eight weeks. God is a healer.

Since the beginning of time, God has expressed his divine desire to heal Israel spiritually, physically, emotionally, and relationally. After one of his greatest feats, the deliverance of Israel from Egyptian bondage by allowing them to crossover the Red Sea, they traveled from the sea side into the wilderness of Shur. It was there where God made them and their descendants a promise. God said, "If you diligently heed the voice of the Lord your God and do what is right in his sight, give ear to his commandments and keep all his statutes, I will put none of the diseases on you which I have brought on the

29

Egyptians; for I am the Lord who heals you." What a tremendous covenant blessing we have with our God. He is Jehovah-Rapha, Yahweh-Rapha, the Lord who heals.

Prayer

Father God, our healer, thank you for serving as our doctor in a sick room, our lawyer in a court room, our counselor in times of confusion, and our friend during seasons of loneliness. Thank you for being our healer in every situation of fear and disease in our body and mind. God thank you for being our healer.

What am I thankful for today?

_____

_____

_____

_____

_____

_____

_____

_____

_____

Day 12

JEHOVAH-JIREH:
"THE LORD WILL PROVIDE"

Genesis 22: 1-19

Just recently, I read a book entitled *The Dead Christian.* The book was written by one of my former students, Wendel Dandridge. Wendel is teaching in the religion department at Clark Atlanta University and serving as the senior pastor of a church he founded called The Worship Center. The thesis for his book is, many Christians are dead because they cannot feel the heartbeat of God. The heartbeat of God is service. Jesus said; "I came into the world not to be served, but to serve." The essence of the book states that contemporary Christian churches are dead because many of them are no longer serving the needs of humankind.

Pastor Dandridge has created a movement among his followers. Consistently, they go out and serve in the community; feeding the hungry, clothing the naked, encouraging those who are inflicted with HIV, ministering to the oppressed and those who are marginalized in society. Young people are joining his ministry each week because they are energized by serving humanity. They are moved by providing for those who are the least of these.

One characteristic of God that fuels his love and concern for us is the fact that he provides for us whatever we need. He is Jehovah-Jireh, God our provider. From the commencement of the spiritual family

Israel, our father Abraham was given the assurance that God would provide for him. Abraham was willing to give God the thing that he loved the most, his only son. God honored the fact that Abraham was faithful in his service, and rewarded him with the promise that he would bless and multiply his descendants, and in his seed, all the nations of the earth would be blessed. Yes, we are grafted into the blessed promise of Abraham.

Prayer

Father God, thank you for providing for us. You are Jehovah-Jireh, Yahweh-Jireh, the Lord who provides for us. And because you are so good to us, help us to share your goodness and your provision with those who are in need. Please give us a heart to serve.

What am I thankful for today?

_____

_____

_____

_____

_____

_____

_____

_____

_____

Day 13

JEHOVAH-NISSI: "THE LORD OUR BANNER"

Exodus 17: 8-16

The current culture in our world is wrought with violence, fear, terrorism, intimidation, oppression, depression, racism, sexism, disease, pestilence, and seemingly, a healthy respect for the righteousness of God is all but disappeared. I write in my book *#God: Religion and the Millennials* a main source of contention among this generation is "theodicy." Theodicy is the term underpinning the question, "Why do bad things happen to good people?" Millennials often grapple with this principle. They question the existence of a God who would continually allow evil to exist in a world and destroy the lives of people that he claims to love and protect. This is certainly a valid fear and contention.

Israel had the same problem. They wanted to stone the prophet Moses because he led them out of Egyptian captivity, and yet brought them to a place of famine. They asked Moses, "Why is it you have brought us up out of Egypt, to kill us and our children and our livestock with thirst?" Moses, being very distraught, sought God for a solution and he was given instruction to go to a rock in Horeb. He was told to speak to the rock, but out of frustration, he struck the rock and water came flowing out.

Shortly after that victory, Amalek, a fierce enemy of Israel, came to destroy them. Moses told Joshua to choose some men to go out and fight the battle, and he would stand on top of the hill with the rod of God in his hand. As long as his hands were raised, Israel would gain an advantage during the battle. But if he let down his hands, Amalek would prevail. When Moses began to get tired, Aaron and Hur went to the top of the hill, put a stone under Moses, got on each side of him and held up his hands. As a result of his hands being lifted, Joshua and Israel defeated Amalek and his army. Moses called the place "The Lord Is My Banner." God promised to give us victory, as long as our hands are raised in praise and honor to his holy name.

Prayer

Father, thank you for being our banner. Thank you for giving us victory in every situation in our lives. The psalmist Jonathan Nelson performed a song entitled "My Name is Victory." Every child of God can be assured that in every situation that we face in life, we are more than conquerors and we always win. Because of Jehovah-Nissi, Yahweh-Nissi, the Lord our victory.

What am I thankful for today?

_____

_____

_____

_____

_____

_____

_____

_____

_____

Day 14

Jehovah-Shalom: "The Lord Our Peace"

Judges 6:11-24: John 14: 25-31

I think the greatest need in the world now is the need for peace. People in the world live in a constant state of fear. They live in fear of losing their jobs, their health, their life savings, their parents, and their children. A very unfortunate occurrence is the fact that a great number of people have lost their hope. Once hope is lost, rejection and despair set in. These two emotional states lead to depression, anger, bitterness, and in many cases, suicidal ideation. Many people in the world just feel like they don't have any reason to continue on with life. What a tragic destination to reach, when a person decides that there is no longer any reason to live.

Jehoveh-Shalom is the God of peace. A relationship with Jesus Christ offers hope and peace to anyone who believes in Him. Jesus said, "Peace I leave with you; my peace I give to you; not as the world gives do I give to you." Real, true peace and contentment can only come from a relationship with God.

Prayer

Father, in a world where there seems to be no peace, thank you for being the prince of peace. Your word declares that, "You will keep him in perfect peace; whose mind is stayed on you, because he trusts in you." God, we have put all our trust in you and therefore we have peace that surpasses all understanding. Thank you for the gift of peace.

What am I thankful for today?

_____

_____

_____

_____

_____

_____

_____

_____

_____

Day 15

JEHOVAH-ROHI: "GOD OUR SHEPHERD"

Psalms 23

One of the greatest revelations I received during my trip to the holy land, Israel, was how a shepherd cares for his sheep. During our tour, we traveled to a sheep field. In the field were several shepherds and hundreds of sheep grazing. When one shepherd would stand up and make a certain distinctive sound, only his particular sheep would respond to that sound and commence to gather for direction. This was an amazing sight and it brought new meaning to the words, "My sheep know my voice."

We, like sheep, have gone astray and we need a shepherd to provide guidance and direction. This psalm of David that depicts the interactions between sheep and his shepherd shows exactly how dependent the sheep are on the shepherd. David said, "I shall not want," meaning every provision is supplied. "He makes me to lie down, he leads me into quiet places; he protects me from the dangers that surround me; he soothes my wounds and he takes care of my every need." As a child of God, what a blessing it is to have the great shepherd leading and guiding us each day.

Prayer

Father, what a great shepherd you are. We are able to rest and trust in you for every provision, everlasting protection, and even a final resting place that we can call home. You are Yahweh-Rohi, the great shepherd. Thank you for allowing dirty, arduous, and wayward sheep to follow you. We appreciate your divine leadership and direction.

What am I thankful for today?

_____

_____

_____

_____

_____

_____

_____

_____

_____

Day 16

FEBRUARY 29, 2016
"A LEAP OF FAITH"

Luke 5: 1-11

Every four years, an extra day is added to the month of February. This is referred to as a leap year. Solar scientists and astrologers have concluded that it takes the earth exactly 365.2422 days to complete an orbit around the sun. So leap year was instituted in 1852 by Pope Gregory VIII as part of the Gregorian calendar, as a way of keeping the time and seasons in sync with the earth and its orbits. I believe that leap year is a great time to take a leap of faith and believe God to so something extraordinary in your life.

It has been said that God uses ordinary people to do extraordinary things. The word declares that "God is able to do exceedingly, abundantly above all that we could ask or think." Even during seasons in our lives when we feel fatigued, frustrated, and forsaken, God can still perform enormous breakthroughs for us. Jesus emphatically delivered this message to the church when he commissioned the disciples for service.

Peter, James and John had been fishing all night and had caught nothing. This was their profession, their trade, their livelihood, their only means of survival, and yet they had failed. Jesus, seeing the discouragement on their faces, enters a boat, pulls up next to Peter and said, "Launch out into the deep and let down your nets for a catch." Jesus was encouraging him to take a leap of faith. Already tired and weary, Peter decided to obey the instruction from the Lord, and as a result, he caught so much fish, that he had to call other boats to help gather the haul. God will always honor the faith and obedience of believers. Are you willing to take a leap of faith?

Prayer

Father, we thank you for being a God who does extraordinary things in our lives. You are always there to encourage and uplift us when we need it the most. You have challenged us to walk by faith and not by sight. As long as we obey your instructions, you will honor our faith by giving us great victory. I encourage all believers to take a leap of faith, especially during leap year.

What am I thankful for today?

_____

_____

_____

_____

_____

_____

_____

_____

_____

_____

Day 17

IN THE BEGINNING WAS THE WORD

John 1: 1-5, 14

How significant is the word of God in your life? One day as I was ministering to my congregation, I told them that, "you will never become what God has created you to become, nor will you receive all that God has for you, until you become a lover of his word."

God's word is so central to the success in our lives as believers. Apostle Paul revealed to us that as children of God, we should not be conformed to this world, but be transformed by the renewing of our minds, that we may prove what is the good, acceptable and perfect will of God. The only way to prove, to be approved, or to become proof of God's will, we must be transformed by his word. David said, "Thy word have I hid in my heart, that I may not sin against God." Heaven and earth will pass away, but the word will stand forever.

The only substantial, substantive, stable foundation available to us today is the word of God. The word was with God in the beginning. The word is alive and present with us each day. The word will be here when we go home to be with the Lord eternally. Every child of God must read, study and develop a devotion to the word of God.

Prayer

Father, we thank you for the word. Thank you for the word becoming flesh and dwelling among men. Thank you for the promise of one day being in the presence of the word forever more. Thy word is a lamp unto our feet and a light on our path. There is life in the word.

What am I thankful for today?

_____

_____

_____

_____

_____

_____

_____

_____

_____

Day 18

YESHUA (JESUS) THE CREATOR?

John 1: 1-5

One of the greatest theological debates that still remain is who actually did the creating? Genesis 1:1 "In the beginning God created the heavens and the earth. The earth was without form and void; and darkness was upon the face of the deep. And the Spirit of God was hovering over the face of the waters." John 1:2, He (Yeshua) was in the beginning with God. All things were made through him, and without him, nothing was made that was made. So who actually did the creating? Was it God, Jesus, or the Holy Spirit?

I think the question is an excellent topic for debate. I believe God created the canvas, Jesus splattered in the details, and the Holy Spirit brought life to it all. Genesis 2:7 "And the Lord God formed man from the dust of the ground, (the canvas) and breathed into his nostrils the breath of life, (the spirit); and man became a living being (God incarnate or God in the flesh). Whoever created the heavens, the earth, mankind and all that dwells therein; it all belongs to God." Who do you believe did the creating?

Prayer

Father, I am eternally grateful just to be a part of this wonderful creation. I appreciate the words of the psalmist when he said, "I will praise you, for I am fearfully and wonderfully made; marvelous are your works, and that my soul knows very well." Psalm 139:14. As long as there is breath in my body, I will praise your holy and righteous name for the great and mighty things that you have done. To God be the glory!

What am I thankful for today?

_____

_____

_____

_____

_____

_____

_____

_____

_____

Day 19

FRESH RAYS OF SON SHINE

1 John 5:1-13

Today is the first day of the month of March. This is a great time of year because for me it signals the commencement of spring. Although spring has not officially begun, when the calendar turns to March, we know that spring is just around the corner. Flowers begin to blossom, trees began to grow leaves, the birds begin to sing, the grass renews its color, and the daylight from the sun rays infuse life into everything breathing.

This is the way it is for God's human creation. It is the Son, Jesus the Christ, that has given us life. John wrote, "And this is the testimony: that God has given us eternal life; and this life is in His Son. He who has the Son has life; he who does not have the Son of God does not have life." Jesus said, "The thief comes to steal, kill and destroy, but I came that you might have life and have it more abundantly." John 10:10. If you know anyone who is dying—dying for love, dying for a quality relationship, dying for healing, dying because of a lack of vision, introduce them to the source of life. God gave his Son, the Son gave his life, that we might have a right to the tree of life. Thank God for a fresh ray of Son shine.

Prayer

Father, thank you for the Son that shines in our lives each day. Without the warmth of the anointing that flows from his being, without the healing virtue that flows from his garment, without the love that emanates in his heart; and without the Son shinning in us, on us, and through us, we could not experience life. Father, we thank you for the blessing of eternal life that comes from your Son.

What am I thankful for today?

_____

_____

_____

_____

_____

_____

_____

_____

_____

Day 20

WHAT DO YOU HAVE TO OFFER?

Psalms 68:19, 103:1-5, 116:12-14

For more than twenty years, I have served as associate professor of Religion at Clark Atlanta University in Atlanta, Georgia. It has been one of my greatest joys to teach, nurture, and train young minds to help prepare them for success in life. One great philosopher stated, "The goal of education is not the mastery of the subject matter, but the mastery of the personhood." The foundation of my teaching philosophy is to not only develop scholars who are prepared for life sustaining opportunities, but to develop people who exhibit high moral excellence and have a strong desire to serve humankind.

Most college students have one main goal for attending college, to get a job. They want the job with the highest starting salary possible. One of the things that I stress to them is, when selecting an employer, do not just consider the base salary, but check out the benefits. A company or organization that offers quality benefits like healthcare, insurance and retirement, these fringe benefits can be just as or even more valuable than the gross salary.

One of the greatest service jobs in the world is working for the kingdom of God. This opportunity not only pays a handsome salary, but the benefits are out of this world. Those who work for God and Son, have you thanked God today for all of his benefits toward you? Have you given him thanks for the benefit of healing, deliverance, counseling, training, prosperity and the power to get wealth? Wow, what an awesome employer to work for and to serve in a company that will never go bankrupt.

Prayer

Father, thank you for all the benefits that you bestow upon us each day. It is such an honor to work for God and Son. There is no greater employer in the world. Thank you for the opportunity to work while it is day, for the night is coming when no man can work.

What am I thankful for today?

_____

_____

_____

_____

_____

_____

_____

_____

_____

Day 21

THE POWER OF THE CROSS

John 19: 17-30

I have often wondered why God placed us on the earth to interact with other people. I believe the reason was to teach us how to bond, how to love, to forgive, and to appreciate the value of God's creation. I think this is the reason we are born into family units, we get married and have children, in order to perpetuate ongoing family ties. It is pretty obvious that God wanted a family. God incarnate was Jesus' birthing in heaven to become God's beloved son. This miracle created a family and was the catalyst for the birthing of more sons and daughters. God birthed children into the world who would carry his nature and continue the work on the earth that the first son had begun.

When human creation lost fellowship with the father because of sin, God wanted to bring them back into righteous relationship with himself, thus the power of the cross. When the first son died for the sins of the other sons and daughters, we were brought back into right relationship with the father. Now we have been reconciled back to "Abba" father, our heavenly father. How is your relationship with the father?

Prayer

Father, we thank you for loving us enough to create a way for your extended family to be reconnected back to you. Thank you for Jesus. Thank you for the resurrection power of the cross. What could have washed away our sins, nothing but the shed blood of Jesus Christ on the cross. Thank God for Calvary.

What am I thankful for today?

_____

_____

_____

_____

_____

_____

_____

_____

_____

Day 22

RESURRECTION CONFIRMED!

Revelation 1:9-20

It is an interesting fact that every time we make a flight, lodging, or car rental reservation, we always request a confirmation number. Sometimes, without us even asking, the attendant will say, "Would you like a confirmation number?" It gives us assurance that we will arrive at our destination, because it has been confirmed. Therefore, we have little doubt that our reservation is complete and the destination is sure.

Jesus gives us a confirmation regarding our anticipated heavenly destination. Throughout the book of Revelation, Jesus confirms that "I am the Alpha and the Omega, the Beginning and the End; who is and who was and who is to come, the Almighty." John calls Jesus the faithful witness "confirmation," the firstborn from the dead, and the ruler over the kings of the earth. Jesus confirms, "I am he who lives and was dead, and behold, I am alive forevermore." "And I have the keys of hell and death." It is a tremendous comfort for us to know that not only has the resurrection been confirmed, but our destiny is sealed unto the day of redemption.

Prayer

Father, thank you for giving us the confirmation code, J-E-S-U-S. All we have to do is have faith and believe on him. This will assure us that we will arrive faithfully at our destination. Thank you God for leading us to our new home and confirming it with your Holy Spirit.

What am I thankful for today?

_____

_____

_____

_____

_____

_____

_____

_____

_____

Day 23

DO YOU LOVE GOD THE WAY YOU ONCE DID?

Revelation 2: 1-7

All of us can remember our first experiences; our first kiss, our first date, our first car, our first house, and especially our first love. It does not matter how long ago it was, you always remember the first time you fell in love with that special someone. How you longed to be in their presence. You just had to talk with them prior to retiring for the day. You could not wait to spend time with them the next day. There was simply no other person in the world that mattered at that time.

For many of us, we remember the day we got saved. We were so excited to know that our sins had been forgiven. We had a brand new relationship in our lives with the one who created us. Many of us joined a local assembly or church and started working on ministries. We were on fire for God and then, what happened? Going to church became routine. Spending time together with God in worship became just an exercise in futility. We had lost our enthusiasm and left our first love.

For this very reason, God chastised the church at Ephesus. Jesus said, "I know your works, your labor, your patience, and that you cannot bear those who are evil. Nevertheless, I have this against you, that you have left your first love." Can God accuse you of not loving him the way you once did? Are you guilty of a lack of communicating with him or no longer enjoying his presence? If this is the case with you, the Lenten season is a good time to repent and do the first works. In other words, rekindle the fire between you and God. His love for you will never diminish. The desire inside of him will never go out.

Prayer

Father, we thank you for continuing to love us just as much as you did when you created us. Help us to rekindle the love that we once had for you. Thank you for being our God and friend, our companion and comforter. Thank you for loving us enough to die for us.

What am I thankful for today?

_____

_____

_____

_____

_____

_____

_____

_____

_____

Day 24

LET SUFFERING BECOME A BLESSING

Revelation 2: 8-11

One of the greatest challenges for a born again believer is to appreciate suffering. God's word is clear that our trials come to make us strong. Count it all joy when you fall into various trials and tribulations, knowing that the trying of your faith brings about patience. We read and hear these words preached all the time, but our faith seems to weaken during our most difficult moments in life.

It can be understandable that a person would lose hope in the midst of a hopeless situation. It could be attributed to human nature that an individual would take on a defeatist attitude in the face of insurmountable odds. However, God's word remains consistent in revealing to us that perseverance in the face of persecution leads to ultimate victory.

God challenged the church at Smyrna to hold on to their faith during their time of persecution. This church was persecuted daily by Jews who joined with pagan believers to put them to death. False Jews who were loyal to Rome and engaged in practices of emperor worship created daily hardships for the believers in Smyrna. In the face of all of that, God told the church to remain faithful in the midst of these trails, and they would receive a crown of life. This was not a crown received after the resurrection; this was a victorious wreath that victors received after defeating their enemy in battle. These crowns are given to those who daily overcome. Always remember, we are more than conquerors through Christ that loved us.

Prayer

Father, we thank you for the daily victories that you grant us in the here and now. Because you have made us more than conquerors, we can get our crowns of life on this side as well as in heaven. If we can hold on and allow our struggles to bring us closer to you instead of drawing us away from you, you have promised to give us the victory.

What am I thankful for today?

_____

_____

_____

_____

_____

_____

_____

_____

_____

Day 25

A Door Has Been Opened for You

Revelation 3: 7-13

When Jesus died on the cross and descended into the abyss of hell, he took the keys from Satan. Now Jesus has all authority. He has the key of David. He has the ability to open the door of salvation and blessings to everyone who will receive and enter.

God revealed to the church at Philadelphia that because of their faithfulness, a door was opened to them. A door that only God could open and no man could close. God has opened a door for you today. In spite of all your trials and tribulations, all your setbacks and disappointments, God is going to bless you because you did not give up. You remained faithful to the call of God that is on your life. Now you are ready to enter into that door of abundant blessings that has been opened for you.

Prayer

Father, thank you for the strength you have given us to remain faithful. Thank you for the open door to salvation and blessings. Thank you for being such a loving and forgiving God. Thank you for being who you are in our lives.

What am I thankful for today?

_____

_____

_____

_____

_____

_____

_____

_____

_____

Day 26

It's Time to Work

James 2: 14-26

Several weeks ago, God revealed to me why the Christian church is on life support and ready for death. The statistics are mortifying as it relates to the number of church closings and the reasons people are leaving the church. The number one reason is the lack of action; the body of Christ is dying because it is lifeless. We are called to carry on the work that the head of the church, Jesus Christ, started. The spirit of the Lord has anointed me to preach the gospel to the poor, to heal the brokenhearted, to minister to those who are captive and help them to recover their sight. I am anointed to liberate those who are oppressed and to tell the world about the coming of the Lord. This is a paraphrase of Luke 4:18. The challenge for the contemporary church is, we are doing very little if any of this commission. We have become derelict in our duties. "And faith without works is dead."

I have challenged my congregation at Friendship Baptist Church in Appling, Georgia, and I will present this same challenge to you. It is time to go to work. What good is our faith if we do not put it into action? Faith without works is dead. Our faith must affect and impact our world. Until the world sees the fruit of our faith, we will continue to be a lifeless corpse, a body with no spirit. Let us become alive again by fulfilling the call to continue the work of Jesus Christ in the earth. The world is waiting for the sons and daughters of God to rise up and work.

Prayer

Father, wake us up to the sense of our duty. Make us a relevant body of believers again. Help us to put our faith into action. Revive us that we might be a blessing to your world. You died to save us, now resuscitate us for your glory. Amen.

What am I thankful for today?

_____

_____

_____

_____

_____

_____

_____

_____

_____

Day 27

THANKFULNESS: THE FUEL TO FAITH

Luke 17: 11-19

When I began writing this Lenten journal, one of the things that I really wanted to emphasize was thanks giving. We celebrate the miracle of Jesus death, burial, and resurrection; but are we really thankful for his sacrifice? I believe thanksgiving or giving thanks is a spiritual discipline most often overlooked. If God desires anything to be revealed from the miracle of Easter, it is the fact that we should always be thankful for God reconciling us back to himself through Christ Jesus. If there is one thing that moves God to action on our behalf, it is our willingness to give thanks.

The miracle healing of the ten lepers speaks volumes concerning our need to be thankful to God. These men were diseased and excommunicated from their society. When they saw Jesus, they shouted for him to heal them. Jesus told them to go show themselves to the priest, and while they were on their way, they were healed. Yet only one of them retuned to give thanks. Jesus asked the Samaritan, "Did I not heal ten? Where are the other nine?"

The word of the Lord to the one who returned to give thanks: "Go in peace, your faith has made you whole." The one who gave thanks received much more than just healing from leprosy, he received the blessing of wholeness. The residual effect of his thankfulness meant that his life was totally complete from any reoccurring physical, mental, or spiritual abnormalities. He was made whole. Giving thanks to God opens the door for complete wholeness and total victory in every area of our lives.

Prayer

Father, we thank you for honoring the heart of the thanks-giver. Thank you for being the reason that we ought to give thanks. Because of all the great and mighty things that you have done in our lives, every day is a day of thanksgiving. A true believer must always give thanks, for this is the will of God in Christ Jesus for you.

What am I thankful for today?

_____

_____

_____

_____

_____

_____

_____

_____

_____

_____

Day 28

FAITH: THE WAY TO SALVATION

Luke 19: 1-10

Many believers have questions regarding what salvation really means. Are we "once saved, always saved?" Is salvation a one-time thing? Is salvation a lifelong process? What is your definition of salvation? When Jesus died for us on the cross, was that all it took to save us? Does the death, burial, and resurrection of Jesus Christ mean that all who believe in him are saved? Does Romans 10 delineate the steps to salvation, "If thou shall confess with thy mouth the Lord Jesus, and believe in thine heart that God hath raised him from the dead, thou shalt be saved." "For with the heart man believeth unto righteousness; and with the mouth confession is made unto salvation." Is the plan of salvation simply confessing and believing? These and many questions fill our hearts as it relates to salvation. However, there is one thing that we can be sure about salvation, it requires love and thanksgiving.

An example of this is Jesus' relationship with a hated sinner; a tax collecting thief and a servant to the Roman government. A simple meeting of the minds can bring about forgiveness and salvation. When Zacchaeus met Jesus, he looked at himself and realized what he had been doing was wrong. He immediately confessed his sins, and made a commitment to return all he had stolen from others. Jesus' response to his act of repentance was, "Today you have received salvation." How simple was that? Zacchaeus just repented from doing wrong and made a commitment to make it right. I believe that this is the simple process of salvation, repent, believe and give thanks.

Prayer

Father, we thank you for the gift of salvation. Thank you for making it so easy for us to receive it. If we just repent and make a commitment to serve you by serving others. What a great gift to mankind. Thank you for saving us.

What am I thankful for today?

_____

_____

_____

_____

_____

_____

_____

_____

_____

_____

Day 29

THE BIRTH DEFECT!

Acts 3: 1-20

One of the greatest blessings a person can receive is to be born without any physical or mental defects. Many children live their entire lives with defects that occurred at birth. Many times, the cause of the birth deformation is not known. Sometimes the cause is known, and occasionally, the defect was caused by a trauma during the birthing process.

I often ask the question, "Is it better to be born with a defect, or to experience a trauma later in life that causes an imperfection of some type in the body?" For instance, contracting an incurable disease, or being involved in a tragic auto accident. Would it be better to have been born blind, than to have had the blessing of sight and lose it for whatever reason? Would it have been better to be born lame, than to have had the blessing of being able to walk, and lose that ability?

Peter and John met a man at the gate called beautiful who had been lame from birth. This man had never experienced the blessing of putting one foot in front of the other and going from point A to point B. He was carried to the gate of the synagogue every day to simply sit and beg for money. One day, Peter and John offered him a solution to his dilemma. The answer to his problem was for him to put faith in the healing power of God. Peter could give him nothing materially but offered him Jesus and then extended his hand. The man took Peter by the hand and immediately, the power of God strengthened the lame man. The man leaped up and started walking into his God ordained destiny.

Prayer

Father, today we thank you for the ability to walk from one place to another. We often take for granted many of our blessings—the blessings of sight, smell, hearing, taste, and touch. Today we thank you for the spiritual, physical, and emotional blessings of life that we enjoy each day. Today we thank you for the little things.

What am I thankful for today?

_____

_____

_____

_____

_____

_____

_____

_____

_____

Day 30

LIFE OR DEATH? YOU CHOOSE

Deuteronomy 30: 11-20

One of the things that I discovered very early in life is that success is largely determined by the choices you make. We are created in the image of God. What makes us unique from any other creation is our ability to choose. Although the creator knows our thoughts before we think them, God gives us the right to choose. The important thing for us to know is that with each choice made, there is a consequence. The result will always bring life or death. God always wants us to choose life.

God spoke to the children in Israel, and his word to them was, "I call heaven and earth as witnesses today against you, that I have set before you life and death, blessing and cursing, therefore choose life that both you and your descendants may live." Sometimes it seems to be a frightening proposition, to have been given the right to choose. Always consider the wisdom of God's word when making a decision. God always has our best interest at heart.

Prayer

Father, today we thank you for the right to choose. You did not give us the spirit of fear, but you gave us love, power, and a sound mind. Help us to make good choices. Help us to choose the life that you have designed for us, a life that will prosper us and bring us peace. I choose life!

What am I thankful for today?

_____

_____

_____

_____

_____

_____

_____

_____

_____

Day 31

Trust the Plan

Jeremiah 29:11

One of the most quoted passages in the bible is Jeremiah 29:11; "I alone know the plans I have for you, plans to bring you prosperity and not disaster, and plans to bring about the future you hope for." What a tremendous blessing to know that the creator of life had a blueprint design for your life. The plan was filled with all the things that he has given us to enjoy life and to prosper. The challenge for us is to trust the plan.

Many times, the vicissitudes of life cause us to doubt God's love and goodness. When tragedy occurs or death takes a loved one, we start to think that God's plan was not as originally designed. We start to feel as though this plan was not what it was designed to be. These are the times when we must trust God's plan the most.

If God be for us, he is more than the whole world against us. Greater is he that is in us than he that is in the world. All things work together for the good for them that love God and are called according to his purpose. Thy words have I hide in my heart that I may not sin against God. Whenever you start to distrust the plan, speak God's word over your life and God's plan will reappear as a trustworthy prospectus for your life.

Prayer

God, we thank you for the plan. Thank you for the life blueprint that was created before the beginning of time. During those seasons in our lives when we begin to lose faith in the design, help us to trust the plan and to remain faithful to your will.

What am I thankful for today?

_____

_____

_____

_____

_____

_____

_____

_____

_____

Day 32

THE TABERNACLE

Exodus 29: 38-46

The Lenten season is a time when we celebrate the death, burial, and resurrection of our Lord and Savior Jesus Christ. It is not often that we trace his beginning back to the original covenant, the Old Testament. The establishment of the tabernacle in 1450 BC was a prophetic projection of the redemptive work that would come in the person of the Messiah.

God's word to Moses was, "Make a tabernacle for me, and I will come and dwell with them." The Apostle John writes in the New Testament, "The word became flesh and dwelled with us." The tabernacle was God's physical place to dwell with men. God came in the flesh, to be with us in the person of Jesus. And now his spirit dwells within us. "And I will write my words on their hearts, and they will be my people and I will be there God." The tabernacle was the place of God's dwelling in the Old Testament. In the new covenant, Jesus is the way, the truth, and the life. Now we are the tabernacle. We are the place where God dwells. It is our responsibility to lift up the savior, and God's spirit will draw people into the kingdom of God. It does not yet appear what we shall be, but one day we will see him just as he is.

Prayer

Father, we thank you for being the way and then making a way for us to dwell with you. Now we can come boldly to the throne of grace and make our petitions known. What a blessing it is to know that there are no barriers blocking our communion with you. Thank you for dwelling in the tabernacle of our hearts.

Day 33

It's Examination Time

2 Corinthians 13: 1-6

We have heard so many life metaphors—life is like a game, play fair; life is not a destination, it's a journey. One thing we know for sure, life teaches us valuable lessons and sometime we are not ready for the test. Preparation and planning is the key to success. There are times in the University of Life when we are not prepared for the exam. The same is true in our walk with God.

Paul admonishes the Corinthian believers to examine themselves to see if they are in the faith. Test yourself! I believe the master teacher has created optimum opportunities for exam preparation. The Lenten Season is one such time when we are challenged to evaluate ourselves in order to prepare for the rededication of our lives to God. In the University of Life, it is beneficial to periodically test yourself to see what you have learned and how you can apply it to your life. The fruits of the spirit are good rubrics to use to evaluate if we are showing evidence of the Holy Spirit's presence in our lives. Do we exhibit love, joy, peace, longsuffering, kindness, goodness, faithfulness, gentleness, self-control. What will be your final grade on the exam?

Prayer

Father, we know that our test and trials come to make us strong. Examining ourselves will only help to better prepare us for successful navigation through the tests of life, and to pass with high marks. Thank you for being such a wonderful teacher and leaving us with a textbook that we can read daily. The B-I-B-L-E, basic instructions before leaving earth.

What am I thankful for today?

_____

_____

_____

_____

_____

_____

_____

_____

_____

_____

Day 34

THE LAW OF BELIEF

Mark 11: 20-24

It seems such a simple thing to declare to a believer, just have faith in God. But the reality is that too many children of God have difficulty trusting God. Our high rate of depression, sickness and disease are evidence that we live our lives in fear and with too much anxiety. God's word is clear that we should not worry about what we will eat, drink, wear, nor worry about any of our physical needs. The God who provides for the sparrows will certainly provide every need that arises in our lives. The challenging question before us is, do we believe?

The Holy Spirit showed me something that I want to share with you. The greatest law in life is the law of belief. Jesus declared on many occasions, "If you can believe, all things are possible to them that believe." To live is to Be-live. Delete the "lie" and be-live. To be alive is to trust God with all your heart, soul and mind. Delete the lie that there is not enough. Delete the lie that says God cannot supply all my needs. Delete the lie that says, what's in the world is greater than what lives on the inside of me. Take out the lie and live, just be-live.

Prayer

Father, we thank you for revealing to us that all things are possible if we just believe. If we remove the lies that have been sown into our hearts, and trust you with all of our heart; there shall be nothing impossible with you in our lives. Lord, we want to believe, but help our unbelief.

What am I thankful for today?

Day 35

SALVATION AND BELIEF

Romans 10: 1-13

As I was sitting in the barbershop today awaiting my weekly haircut, God showed me something about the process regarding the law of belief. Our very salvation, or what Paul would refer to as the steps to salvation, follows this same process. Believe, speak, and receive. Salvation is the act of believing, speaking, and receiving.

The word is in your mouth and in your heart. That if you confess with your mouth the Lord Jesus and believe in your heart that God raised him from the dead, you will be saved. How appropriate it is to live our lives based on the very law that secured our salvation. Believe in your heart and speak it with your mouth, and you can have whatever you say. The law of belief is what governs our prayer life. "Whatever you ask God for when you pray, believe and you will have them."

Prayer

Father, thank you for giving us the process for obtaining success in life—believe, speak and receive. Today, I believe that you will comfort and sustain my family during the passing of my cousin Gerald. Please bless his family and our extended family during this difficult time. I believe that you will restore to us the joy that was lost.

Dedicated to the memory of my cousin, Winston Gerald Howard (1973-2016) RIP.

What am I thankful for today?

_____

_____

_____

_____

_____

_____

_____

_____

_____

_____

Day 36

I Am No More a Sinner

Romans 5: 6-20

I believe one of the greatest challenges in the body of Christ is the lack of understanding regarding the grace of God. Grace has been defined as, "God's unmerited favor." Many Christians fail to realize the significant power and meaning of grace. We were saved by grace through faith, which was a gift from God. The salvation grace of God bought our pardon from sin and made us the righteousness of God. Now, instead of declaring that you are a sinner, you should declare that you are the righteousness of God. This transformation was brought about by the grace of God.

The Apostle Paul writes, "But God commended his love toward us, in that, while we were yet sinners, Christ died for us." The blood soaked cross of Calvary freed us from the power and control of sin. Now we have been justified by faith through Christ, and freed from the guilt stain of sin. We are a new creation. Old things are passed away, and all things have become new.

Now, let us walk in righteousness. You have been saved by grace. You don't have to try and do anything in order to make yourself righteous. God has finished that work on the cross. Now you can rightfully say, I am no more a sinner, I am the righteousness of God.

Prayer

Father, how grateful we are for the completed work of Christ on the cross. Thank you for making us righteous. I am no longer a sinner. I am a righteous person. I am grateful that I have received all the benefits of living in righteousness.

What am I thankful for today?

_____

_____

_____

_____

_____

_____

_____

_____

Day 37

A BRAND NEW LIFE

Romans 6: 1-14

One of the questions raised by many millennials is, "Is baptism a requirement in order to be a Christian?" Baptism is simply a symbolic ritual performed by most, if not all forms, of religion. In Christianity it symbolizes the death, burial, and resurrection of Jesus the Christ. Being submerged under water and raised up out of the water is simply an outward demonstration of an inward confession. An individual has symbolically been cleansed from an old way of living, and has made a decision to start a new life.

Paul describes this symbolic act like this: "Therefore we are buried with him by baptism into death: that like as Christ was raised up from the dead by the glory of the father, even so we also should walk in newness of life." My ninety-three-year-old grandma used to say to me, "You can go down a dry devil and come up a wet one!" However, if an individual has repented from sin and made a confession that God has raised Jesus from the dead, he has received salvation and has become a new creation. He now has a brand new life in Christ.

Prayer

Father, we thank you for making a way for us to become a new creation. Thank you for allowing us to repent, change our way of thinking, and go in a new direction. Thank you for the transforming power of faith and grace through Jesus Christ. Because he lives, we can face tomorrow walking in a brand new life.

What am I thankful for today?

_____

_____

_____

_____

_____

_____

_____

_____

_____

Day 38

There is Safety in God's Love

Romans 8:31-39

The world that we live in today is a very scary place. We are living in the last days. God's word warns us that during that time, there would be famines, pestilences, lawlessness will abound, and the love of many would grow cold. I don't believe that Jesus could have even envisioned what we are seeing happen today. In the city of Atlanta, Georgia, nearly eight teenagers have been brutally murdered this week. Most of the deaths were attributed to gun violence. There were two college-bound high school seniors who were beaten to death by a twenty-year-old male. It is really sad to see so many young people losing their lives while many more are throwing their lives away.

It hit home for us in our ministry as we lost a member of our congregation; eighteen years old, robbed, and killed senselessly. I watched this young man grow up in our church, and I witnessed the pain on the face of his family as we celebrated his life. He left this world far too soon before his dreams and aspirations could materialize.

The word of God is the only thing that can sustain us and bring comfort to our hearts in times like these. Like the Apostle Paul, it takes a strong-willed determination not to allow anything to separate you from the love of God. When tragedy strikes our lives, it is very difficult to feel the love of God. However, we must always be persuaded that neither tribulation or distress, death or life, principalities or powers, things present or things to come, will be able to separate us from God's love. It is a real blessing to know that there is safety in God's love.

Prayer

Father, we thank you for shielding and protecting us during these perilous times. Thank you for being our comforter, friend, and guide when things happen that we just don't understand. Thank you for being that hiding place for our souls in the time of trouble. Father, comfort, heal, and bless all the families that have had to deal with the loss of a child. Our prayer is that we will see our loved ones again in that great resurrection morning.

Dedicated to the life and memory of De'Andre Palmer. Gone but not forgotten.

What am I thankful for today?

_____

_____

_____

_____

_____

_____

_____

_____

Day 39

RECONCILED TO GOD

Matthew 6: 25-34

As we approach the ending of this forty-day Lenten journey of thanksgiving, we are yet reminded that Jesus was our first sacrifice. Because he gave his life for us, we have been given the opportunity to be reconciled back to God and gain the privilege of eternal life.

If we always remember to give back to God first and to our brothers and sisters in community, everything we need will be given to us and much more. If we make God the priority of our lives and keep our focus on heaven, we will enjoy the blessings of God. God desires to have first place in our lives. The first commandment given to Israel was, "Have no other gods before me." If we keep God first and strive for righteousness, what a wonderful world this would be. Moreover, what a lifetime of joy, peace and thanksgiving will be ours because of our sharing with others.

Prayer

Father, what a blessing it was for you to give us your son as the first born among many brethren. The old song lyrics are ringing out in my spirit: "God gave his son, the son gave his life, that we might have a right to the tree of life." Father, thank you for the gift of reconciliation. Thank you for making us the righteousness of God in Christ.

What am I thankful for today?

_____

_____

_____

_____

_____

_____

_____

_____

_____

Day 40

It is Finished!

John 19: 28-30

Wow, I started this Lenten journey several months ago. I have had this vision in my heart for some time. God spoke to me in January, 2016 and said, "Write the vision, and make it plain, so they who read it may run with it and be blessed." This forty-day Lenten journal will be one of reflection, revival, renewal and thanksgiving. My prayer is that you were challenged, enlightened, and moved in your heart to make every day a day of thanksgiving.

I want to thank God for the vision and the inspiration. I thank him for the time and the season that was given for me to write. I thank God for the ability and the love that I have for his word. I thank God for the passion that I have to bless, inspire, educate, and appreciate his creation. Now that it is finished, it has just begun.

Now it is your turn to give thanks to God for all the wonderful things that God has done for you. Thank God particularly for the gift of salvation that was so freely given to us by grace and faith in his son Jesus. Thank God for his broken body and his shed blood on the cross at Calvary. Thank God for the final declaration made on our behalf, "It is finished."

Prayer

Father, we thank you one last time in the sacred space of this sanctuary. We offer you our thanksgiving. We are so thankful for your love and kindness. We are so grateful for who you are in our lives. God, continue to lead, guide, and protect us in a world that hated you and hates us as well. We are forever thankful for your presence in our lives. We are thankful to you for giving us your son to die in our place.

What am I thankful for today?

_____

_____

_____

_____

_____

_____

_____

_____

_____

About the Author

For more than twenty years Dr. Philip Dunston has served as a professor of religious studies at Clark Atlanta University and lead pastor/teacher of the Friendship Baptist Church in Appling, Georgia. Dr. Dunston has taught and ministered throughout the United States, Virgin Islands, and South Africa. He has written in scholarly journals and authored a chapter in *Keep it Real, Working with Today's Black Youth*, 2005. Dr. Dunston is currently working on another book, *#God, Religion, Spirituality and Mental Health among Millennials*. He has received numerous academic awards for quality mentoring and teaching and he is leading a tremendously vibrant and progressive ministry in the Central Savannah River Area of Georgia.